Discover Your Hispanic Heritage

Norma P. Flores

HERITAGE BOOKS
2026

HERITAGE BOOKS

AN IMPRINT OF HERITAGE BOOKS, INC.

Books, CDs, and more—Worldwide

For our listing of thousands of titles see our website
at
www.HeritageBooks.com

Published 2026 by
HERITAGE BOOKS, INC.
Publishing Division
5810 Ruatan Street
Berwyn Heights, MD 20740

International Standard Book Number
Paperbound: 978-0-7884-5547-6

About the Author

My Inspiration to write to "Discover Your Hispanic Heritage"

From a young age, I was captivated by the stories of my ancestors, a fascination sparked at just eleven years old. My journey began with conversations with my parents, my grandparents and my great-grandmother, Maria Esperanza Rodriguez Menchaca. Their tales of life in Eagle Pass, Texas, and across the border in Piedras Negras, Coahuila, ignited a lifelong passion for uncovering our family's roots. This book, "Discover Your Hispanic Heritage" is a reflection of that passion and a guide for anyone embarking on their own genealogical quest. Whether you're just starting or have already delved into your family's past, I hope these pages offer you the tools, insights, and inspiration to connect with your heritage and explore the rich tapestry of Hispanic ancestry. I hope to provide you with fast-track resources and guidance so you can start your family history journey.

Biography of Norma Patricia Flores

Norma Patricia Flores was born in Eagle Pass, Texas, but her early life took a significant turn when her family moved to San Jose, California, shortly after her birth. At just three months old, Norma was brought to San Jose by her father, Daniel Abraham Flores, a distinguished U.S. Army 82nd Airborne Paratrooper. Joining him was Norma's mother, Maria Antonieta Garcia Venegas, who had emigrated from

Valparaiso, Zacatecas, Mexico. Settling in San Jose, the Flores family began to lay down roots in their new community, with Daniel finding employment at General Motors in Fremont.

As the family expanded with the addition of four more siblings, Norma's upbringing was marked by the values of hard work and dedication. These principles guided her educational and professional journey. She pursued higher education at San Jose State University, where she laid the foundation for her future career.

Norma devoted 30 years of her life to the field of education. Her career was characterized by a deep commitment to student welfare and academic excellence. She ultimately achieved the position of Director of Student Services at a local school district, a role in which she made a lasting impact on the educational landscape before retiring.

Norma Patricia Flores's life reflects a dedication to service and education, influenced by her family's immigrant roots and her own pursuit of academic and professional excellence.

In addition, ResearchLatino.com is a Startup company located in Silicon Valley founded by Norma Flores, who has been an avid genealogist for 40 years and Coauthor of "A Beginner's Guide to Hispanic Genealogy". The main goal for the site is to create the largest online subscription based Hispanic genealogy network service. Subscribers will be able to invite family and friends to help build their family trees. Research Latino (RL) hopes to accomplish this mission through collaborations with real-time online genealogists, historians, archivists, surname experts, among other reliable sources that will be key collaborators in providing end-users with the information they desire.

Dedication

To my Dearest Parents,

Daniel Abraham Flores and Maria Antonieta Garcia

This book is a testament to the enduring love, guidance, and unwavering support you have given me throughout my life. Your encouragement has been the foundation on which my dreams have flourished, and for that, I will forever be grateful.

I also wish to honor the 132 ancestors I have uncovered so far, whose lives form the intricate tapestry of my heritage. Their journeys—marked by resilience, love, triumph, and hardship—continue to inspire me, shaping not only who I am today but the legacy I hope to leave behind.

To my grandparents, whose stories, wisdom, and sacrifices have been passed down through the generations, I offer my deepest thanks. It is from your words and lives that my passion for family history first ignited, and this work is, in many ways, a tribute to you.

This book was created with the hope that others will find their own ancestors, connect with their heritage, and pass on the rich legacies of their families to future generations.

Finally, I extend my heartfelt appreciation to the Empire Publishing team. Your steadfast dedication, creativity, and support have made this dream a reality. Working alongside such a talented and committed group has been a privilege, and I am forever grateful for your guidance on this journey.

Norma Flores

Daniel Abraham Flores and Maria Antonieta Garcia

Table of Contents

Introduction 1

Chapter 1: Foundations of Hispanic Genealogy 4

Chapter 2: Hispanic Family History Research Checklist... 7

Chapter 3: Find Your Local Family History Center......... 11

Chapter 4: Navigating Hispanic Records 13

Chapter 5: International Research 92

Chapter 6: Using Technology and Online Resources 96

Chapter 7: Directory of Ethnic Groups 114

Chapter 8: Overcoming Common Challenges 118

Chapter 9: Genealogy Tools Must Haves 124

Introduction

Purpose of the Book: "A Guide to Your Hispanic Heritage" plays a significant role in offering a practical, streamlined approach to tracing Hispanic ancestry. Its focus on fast-track resources is particularly valuable for individuals who may feel overwhelmed by the complexity of genealogical research. By offering clear, actionable steps and highlighting accessible tools and databases, helping readers dive into their Hispanic family history more efficiently.

Additionally, the book can serve as a bridge for connecting people to their cultural roots, allowing them to understand the history, traditions, and stories that have shaped their heritage. For Hispanic lineage, this knowledge is essential in preserving cultural identity across generations, and a fast-track guide helps make that journey easier.

Overview of Hispanic Heritage: Hispanic heritage is a rich and multifaceted tapestry that reflects centuries of cultural blending, historical events, and diverse traditions spanning across Latin America, Spain, and the broader Iberian Peninsula. The term "Hispanic" encompasses people with origins in Spanish-speaking countries, whose histories are intertwined with Indigenous, African, and European roots.

Historically, Hispanic heritage traces back to the Spanish colonization of the Americas, beginning in the 15th century. The colonial period saw a complex exchange of cultures, as Spanish settlers, Indigenous populations, and enslaved Africans contributed to the development of unique traditions, languages, and societal structures. This blending of influences is evident in the architecture, cuisine, music, and festivals of modern-day Hispanic cultures.

Throughout Latin America and Spain, there are deeply rooted customs, family structures, and religious traditions, primarily influenced by Catholicism, yet adapted and transformed in various regions. The Indigenous peoples of the Americas, with their own ancient civilizations such as the Aztec, Maya, and Inca and many more Indigenous nations, continue to play a vital role in the preservation of Hispanic heritage. African heritage, introduced through the Atlantic slave trade, also significantly shaped the cultural and social fabric of Hispanic societies, particularly in the Caribbean and Brazil.

In the United States, Hispanic heritage plays an important role in shaping the nation's identity. With over 60 million people of Hispanic descent, the community reflects a vast range of experiences, languages, and backgrounds. From Mexico, Puerto Rico, and Cuba to countries throughout Central and South America, U.S. Hispanic communities are diverse yet united by common linguistic and cultural threads.

Hispanic genealogy is, therefore, a fascinating journey that involves tracing family lineages across continents and uncovering stories of migration, resilience, and cultural preservation. Understanding this heritage helps individuals connect with their ancestral past and recognize the broad influences that have shaped Hispanic identity across generations. By exploring genealogical records, oral histories, and historical documents, people can gain a deeper appreciation of their place within this vast and diverse Hispanic heritage.

Chapter1

Foundations of Hispanic Genealogy

Getting Started:

Understanding the foundation of Hispanic genealogy begins with recognizing the deep, diverse history of Hispanic cultures across Spain, Latin America, and beyond. The roots of many Hispanic families can be traced through colonial archives, Catholic church records, and civil registrations, all of which provide valuable insights into lineage. In the digital age, genealogists now have access to a wealth of online resources that streamline this research. Platforms like FamilySearch, MyHeritage, and Ancestry offer extensive databases of Hispanic records, with a primary focus on Hispanic Ancestry specialized sites such as PARES (Portal de Archivos Españoles), Archivo General de la Nacion (Portal de Archivos Mexicanos) and focus on Spanish and Latin American documents. Additionally, social media groups and forums dedicated to Hispanic genealogy create a collaborative space where enthusiasts share tips, resources, and personal discoveries, making it easier than ever to uncover and preserve one's Hispanic heritage. Recommended books, websites, archives, and organizations for Hispanic genealogy, (See Chapter 6 Resources)

- **Resources**

This category encompasses a wide range of tools and materials useful for genealogical research. It includes historical documents, databases, software, books, and online platforms that provide access to records like birth, marriage, and death certificates, census data, and immigration records. Resources are essential for anyone seeking to piece together their family history. Recommended books, websites, archives, and organizations for Hispanic genealogy.

- **Libraries and Archives**

Libraries and archives are treasure troves of historical documents and records. They house collections of manuscripts, photographs, newspapers, and official records that are invaluable for genealogical research. Many libraries and archives have specialized collections focused on Hispanic history and genealogy, offering unique insights into the lives and stories of Hispanic ancestors.

- **Genealogy Blogs**

Genealogy blogs are online platforms where enthusiasts and experts share stories, research tips, and insights about tracing family histories. They often focus on specific topics like DNA testing, research methodologies, and cultural heritage. For Hispanic genealogy, these blogs provide a space to explore and discuss the unique challenges and opportunities in researching Hispanic ancestry.

- **Genealogical Societies**

Genealogical societies are organizations dedicated to the study and promotion of genealogy. They offer resources, support, and networking opportunities for both amateur and professional genealogists. Many societies focus on specific regions or cultural groups, providing valuable resources and expertise for those researching Hispanic ancestry. They often host events, workshops, and conferences to facilitate knowledge sharing and community building.

Chapter 2

Hispanic Family History Research Checklist

Gather What You Already Know

Write down family names, birthplaces, and significant dates (births, marriages, deaths).

Ask family members for stories, documents, and photos.

Locate Family Records

Birth/Marriage/Death Certificates – Check for names, dates, places, and any additional notes.

Baptismal and Church Records – Parish records often include early life events.

Family Heirlooms – Examine old letters, Bibles, or keepsakes for clues.

Understand Hispanic Naming Conventions

Familiarize yourself with the two-surname system (e.g., paternal + maternal last names).

Know that first names may include religious or ceremonial additions (e.g., María, José).

In many instances I was able to locate ancestors by simply adding Maria or Jose to their first name.

Research Geographic Origin

Pinpoint towns or regions where ancestors lived (Spain, Mexico, Central/South America).

Look into local histories or geography that may help explain migrations or name changes.

Search Historical Immigration Records

Explore Ellis Island, or other entry ports.

Check Border Crossing Records if family entered the U.S. via Mexico.

Use Spanish-Language Resources (Google translate is helpful in translating Spanish websites into English)

Civil Registration Records – In many Hispanic countries, these are rich in detail.

Catholic Church Archives – Parish registers (baptisms, marriages, burials) hold important data.

Leverage DNA Testing

Consider taking a DNA test to uncover genetic matches in Hispanic communities.

Use GEDmatch, 23&Me or AncestryDNA for deeper connection with Hispanic relatives. Utilize Hispanic Genealogy Websites like MexicanGenealogy.com or new upcoming site Researchlatino.com

FamilySearch.org – Free access to Hispanic-specific databases.

Ancestry.com – Paid service with large collections from Spain and Latin America.

After using 23 & Me and Ancestry DNA I was able to connect with long lost relatives.

Hispanic Genealogical Society Websites – Regional groups may have specialized resources.

Know the Historical Context

Learn about relevant historical events (colonization, migration patterns, wars) affecting your family's movements Research border changes, political shifts, or records destruction in ancestral countries.

Keep a Research Log

Document your sources, findings, and dead ends.

Stay organized with research notes to avoid duplicating efforts.

Stay Consistent with Dates, Names and Spellings

Be aware that Hispanic names may be misspelled or altered in U.S. records.

Look for variations in spelling and abbreviations (e.g., García vs. Garza, Juan vs. J.).

Explore Dual Citizenship Opportunities

Consider Genealogy Supplies, Family Charts, Generation Charts etc at EasyGenie.org or Amazon.com

Chapter 3

Find Your Local Family History Center

Steps for Utilizing a Family History Center (FHC) now renamed Family Search Centers:

Visit the FamilySearch.org website and use their locator tool to find an FHC near you. Most centers are hosted within LDS church buildings but are open to the public.

Check the hours of operation since each center may have different hours depending on staff availability.

Prepare Before You Visit

Gather the information you already have names, dates, places, family records, and documents.

Make a list of specific questions or roadblocks in your research to maximize your time at the FSC.

Set up a free FamilySearch account at FamilySearch.org if you don't already have one. This account is necessary to access many online resources, including FHC-specific databases.

What to Expect at the FSC

Access to <u>FamilySearch Databases</u>: Family History Centers provide free access to premium genealogy websites like <u>Ancestry</u>, <u>MyHeritage</u>, <u>Findmypast</u>, <u>GenealogyBank</u>, and more.

Personalized Assistance: Volunteers are typically available to guide you through your research, help with using the software, and answer questions.

Microfilm and Microfiche: Many FSCs still have collections of microfilm, which are often records that are not yet digitized.

Volunteers at the FSC will be more than glad to teach you how to use a microfilm machine, super simple. I found it easy to use and helpful in my ancestor search. It was truly amazing to read documents through Microfilm. It is worth a visit.

I was a co-founder of The Santa Clara County Genealogical & Historical Society of Santa Clara County in the early 90's. Our members volunteered one day a week at our local Family History Center to help anyone researching their family history

Chapter 4

Navigating Hispanic Records

Navigating Hispanic genealogy documents can be a rewarding yet challenging endeavor, often due to the unique historical, cultural, and linguistic factors involved.

Understanding the Unique Challenges

Language Barriers: Many Hispanic historical records are written in Spanish or other indigenous languages. While translation tools can be helpful, understanding the nuances of these languages can significantly enhance your research.

Record Variations: Record-keeping practices varied across different regions and time periods within Hispanic countries. This can make it challenging to locate specific documents or understand their contents.

Limited Digitization: Not all Hispanic historical records have been digitized, making access to original documents necessary for in-depth research. Make sure to check with country of origin before you head out to the town your ancestors are from, many have original records in old books that may or may not be accessible. I was in Guerrero, Coahuila, Mexico and the town had old civil and church records in regular boxes at a designated persons home to be the keeper of these old documents. They were kind enough to give me access to read them, but with very limited time. Good idea to be informed before visiting ancestral homeland.

Key Document Types to Explore

1. Vital Records

Civil Registration: Civil records (birth, marriage, and death) are key for tracing ancestors. These records became common in Latin American countries and Spain after the late 19th century. Each country has its own civil registration archives.

Mexico: Registro Civil (Civil Registry) began in 1859.

Spain: Registro Civil de España began in 1871.

Other Latin American countries: Many started in the 1800s, but availability may vary.

Church Records: Baptism, marriage, and burial records, especially before the 1800s, are often held by the Catholic Church. Parishes, diocesan archives, and bishops' archives are invaluable.

Spain: Diocesan Archives and local parish archives.

Latin America: Catholic Church archives vary by region, but many are centralized.

2. FamilySearch

FamilySearch.org is one of the largest free resources for international Hispanic genealogy research. Their database includes millions of indexed records from Spain, Mexico, and many other Latin American countries, covering:

Parish and Civil Registries: These records, often kept by churches or government offices, contain information about births, marriages, and death

Census Records: Censuses provide a snapshot of the population at specific points in time, including demographic information and household composition.

Military Records: Military service records can reveal details about a person's life, including their place of birth, family members, and service history.

Church Records: Parish registers, baptismal records, and marriage certificates can be invaluable sources of information about family relationships and religious affiliations.

Land Records: Land ownership records can provide clues about a family's economic status and location.

3. Archival Resources

Spain: Spain has numerous archives, including:

Archivo General de Indias (Seville): Colonial records about Spanish America.

Archivo General de la Nación (Madrid): Historical documents, military, and emigration records.

Provincial Archives: Each province in Spain has its own archives with genealogical records.

Latin America: Key national archives include: **Archivo General de la Nación in Argentina, Colombia, Peru, Mexico, etc., which house historical records and immigration data.**

4. Immigration and Emigration Records

Spanish and Latin American migrations often left detailed records. Look for passenger lists, naturalization records, and immigration data.

Spain to Latin America: Emigrantes a las Indias (Emigrants to the Americas) lists settlers moving to the New World from the 1500s to the 1800s.

Ellis Island/USA Records: If your ancestors emigrated to the U.S., Ellis Island and U.S. naturalization records may contain clues.

Mexico to the U.S Border crossing records

5. Genealogical Societies

Hispanic Genealogical Research Center of New Mexico: Focused on Spanish, Mexican, and Native American genealogy.

The Society of Hispanic Historical and Ancestral Research (SHHAR): Great for research assistance and sharing resources related to Spain, Mexico, and Latin American countries.

Research Strategies

Learn Spanish. Even a basic understanding of Spanish or other relevant languages can greatly improve your research capabilities.

Connect with Other Researchers: Join genealogy forums or societies focused on Hispanic heritage. Collaborating with other researchers can lead to valuable discoveries and insights.

Consider Professional Help: If you're facing significant challenges or need expert guidance, consider hiring a professional genealogist specializing in Hispanic research.

Glossary of Spanish Terms and Definitions of Spanish and English Terms

Here's a breakdown of a glossary of Spanish terms to aid in reading Spanish documents. Key Terms: Includes frequently used words and phrases that might be familiar in many of the documents you may come across.

Spanish	English
Abuelos paternos fueron	Paternal grandparents were
A la pretensa sabín que	At the presence they knew
A los cinco dias del mes	At the fifth day of the month
A quienes advertí	Whom I advised
A quienes advirtió	Whom he advised
A quienes hice saber	Whom I informed
A quién puse por nombre	Who did I name
Amonestó en tres días festivos	Admonished on three holy days
Amonestación	Matrimonial proclamation (Matrimonial proclamation published during three

	successive Sundays before marriages; banns.)
Asistí en el matrimonio de	I assisted in the marriage of
Asistió al matrimonio de	He assisted at the marriage of
Bajo de coro cruz alta	Under the joint high cross
Yo bautice solemnemente	I baptized solemnly
Yo bautice a un párvulo de cuatro	I baptized a four-day-old infant
Yo bautice una párvula de días de Nacido cinco días de nacida	I baptized a five-day-old infant
Bautice solemnemente, puso oleo	I baptized solemnly, put oil

Me casé y cubri con permiso a y crisma este feligrés	I married and veiled with Chrism permission this parishioner
Como cura interino	The interim priest
Con el mutuo consentimiento	With the mutual consent
Con licencia del señor cura	With permission of the priest
Con su mutuo consentimiento	With their mutual consent
Confesados	Having confessed
Conforme al concilio de Trento	Consistent with the council of Trent
Creada y nacida en este suelo	Born and raised on this ground

De esta jurisdicción y su partido	Of this jurisdiction and its district
De este lugar y su Partido	Of this place and its district
De los pretendientes	Of the candidates
De que doy fe	Of which I certify
Desposo por palabra de presente a	Married at the present word
Dias festivos	Holidays
Diligencias Matrimoniales	Marriage vows
El cura	The parish priest
El Licenciado	The lawyer
El párroco	The person
El presbitero	The priest

El teniente	The deputy
El vicario	The vicar
En constancia lo firme	In witness thereof I sign it
El dicho día, mes, y año	On the said day, month, and year
En el curato de	In the parish of
En el dia de la fecha	On this date
En el establecida de la compania precidial	In the establishment of presidial company
En el expresado día, mes, y año	On the expressed day, month, and year
En el pueblo de	In the town of
En el valle de	In the valley of
En la capilla de	In the chapel of
En la ciudad de	In the city of

En la doctrina de	In the doctrine of
En la iglesia de	In the church of
En la parroquia de	In the parish of
En la villa de	In the village of
Encargado	In charge
Enterrado al curato del pueblo	Buried in the village parish
Entrerrado en el cemeterio	Buried at the cemetery
Examinados en la doctrina Cristiana	Examined in Christian doctrine
Exorcice	Exorcise
Falleció en este real	Died in this district
Fiesta de los santos	Festival of the saints
Fueron sus padrinos	They were his godparents

Fueron testigos al tiempo	They were witnesses to the time
Habiéndose amonestado en tres días festivos	Having been admonished on three holidays
Habiendo preguntado a ambos y tenido su mutuo consentimiento	Having asked both of them and had their mutual consent
Habiendo presidido lo dispuesto por el santo concilio de	Having presided over the provisions of the holy council of
Hija legítima de	Legitimate daughter of
Hija natural de	Natural born daughter of
Hijo de la iglesia	Child of the church
Hijo legítimo de	Legitimate son of

Hizo memoria testamentaría aun con todas las formalidades	He made a testamentary memory even with all the formalities
Indios de la nación	Indians of the nation
En misa solemne	In solemn mass
Leídas las tres amonestaciones conciliarías	Read the three conciliar warnings
Aconsejé a estos padrinos de la obligación	I advised these godparents of the obligations
Les aconsejé	I advised them
Originario de esta mineral	Originally from this mineral area
No se le adminstró ningún sacramento	He was not given any sacraments
Padre no conocido	Unknown father

En testimonio de ello lo firmo	In witness thereof I sign it
Para que conste lo firmé	For the record I signed it
En verdad por eso lo firmé	In truth therefore I signed it
Pongo el aceite santa y el crisma sagrado	I put the holy oil and sacred chrism
Esto constituye el verdadero y legítimo matrimonio	This constitutes a true and legitimate marriage
Sagradamente bautizó un niño varón con aceite santo	Sacredly baptized a male child with holy oil
Sacramento de penitencia	Sacrament of penitences
Según el rituales romano	According to the Roman rituals

Sin ningún impedimento para el matrimonio resultante	Without any impediment to the resulting marriage
Sus obligaciones de enseñarle la doctrina Cristiana	Their obligations of teaching them Christian doctrine
Teniente de cura	Deputy of the parish priest
Un hijo varón	A male child
Vecino de este real	Neighbors of the district
Y de padre no conocido	And of unknown father
Y demás obligaciones Cristianas	And other Christian obligations
No haber resultado en ningún impedimento para el matrimonio	Having resulted in no impediment to the marriage

Padre desconocido/misterio	Father unknown/mystery
Y relación espiritual	And spiritual relationship
Y teniendo su mutuo consentimiento	And having his mutual consent
Yo, el presbitero	I, the presbyter

Term	Meaning
abuela	grandmother
abuelo	grandfather
abuelastra	step-grandmother
abuelastro	step-grandfather
adelantado	colonial discoverer
administración	administration
adulterio	adulterer

adviento	advent, the four weeks preceding Christmas
afinidad	relation by marriage
albacea	will executor
alcalde	mayor
alcaldía	Mayor in Colonial New Spain, the crown-appointed mayor of a town that was not a provincial capital.
alcalde ordinario	town council official
aldea	village, hamlet
alferez	standard bearer of a town or expedition
alma	soul, person
almoneda	public auction; clearance sale
alteza	your highness. An honorary title given to the kings, princes, and officials of the

	high court and some of the royal councils.
amparo	Spaniard protector of Indians
anima	soul; spirits consigned to purgatory
año bisiesto	leap year
año secular	centenary years
ante	before, in front of, in the presence of
antiguo/gua	old
apartamiento	judicial act or declaration by which one removes oneself from legal action or right.
apodo	nickname
apostólico	apostolic
appellido	surname, family name, last name
aprendizaje	apprenticeship

aprendizo/za	apprentice, beginner
arancel	official tariff
arcediano	archdeacon
archivo	archive, place where archives are kept
arrendamiento	rent, letting, lease
arroyo	small rivulet
artículo	article
arzobispado	archbishopric; ecclesiastical territory under the jurisdiction of an archbishop
arzobispo	archbishop. The bishop of a metropolitan church to which other bishops are subordinate.
ascendencia	ascendancy
asesor	legal advisor
asiento	seat on a tribunal or council
audiencia	regional high court

ausente	absent, absentee, missing person
ausente sin licencia	(military) absent without leave
auto	judicial sentence, warrant, edict
autos de bienes de difuntos	processing of assets of the deceased
auto de fe	a public procedure in which those accused by the Inquisition were sentenced.
ayuntamiento	town council
bando	marriage banns
bautizar	to baptize, to christen
barranca	ravine or gorge
barrio	district within a city
beneficio	a mining enterprise or mill
bienes de difunto	holdings of legal heirs

bisabuelo/la	great-grandparent
bisnieto/ta	great-grandchild
bolsón	a large region appearing on maps in the shape of a money bag, located in Chihuahua, Durango, and Coahuila.
braza	length or measurement (typically six feet)
bula	papal bull or proclamation
caballería	military cavalry, knightly order, knights
caballero	nobleman, knight, member of military order
cabeza	head
cabildo	municipal or town council
cabildo abierto	meetings of the town council and the citizens of the town.

cacicazo	territory governed by and/or the authority of a Cacique.
cacique	a native chief
cambio	change, exchange, alteration
cantón	jurisdiction of government between municipality and state (late nineteenth and early twentieth-century Mexico).
capellán	a priest with a chaplaincy or who says mass in a private chapel, paid by a trust fund or individual to administer said fund or individual's affairs.
capellanía	benefice or foundation subject to certain obligations.
capillo	invitation for a wedding or baptism

capital	assets, principal of a trust fund
Capitán General	supreme commander of a military region.
capitanía general	territorial demarcation governed by a Captain General during the colonial era.
capitulación	royal agreement between the crown and a conquistador.
casa solar	ancestral home, manor
casado/da	married
casamiento	marriage, wedding
casas reales	government buildings
casta	caste, lineage
castizo	of a good caste
catastro	census of land of a country

catederal/catedra	episcopal church (of a diocese or archdiocese)
caudillo	military leader
cedula	royal decree, document, manuscript
cedula personal/documento	identity card, identification papers
cementerio	cemetery
censo	census of a population
certificación	certification, attestation
cerro	small hill
ciudad	city
ciudadano	citizen; a title given to all persons who appeared before the civil register.
clase	class; type; kind
clérigo	clergyman

cobdicilio	codicil (an addition or supplement to a will)
cofradía	congregation, brotherhood of religious individuals, guild, trade union
colector	tax collector, or collector for the church
colegiata	collegiate church
colegio notarial	notarial college
colonial	time period beginning at the Spanish conquest and ending with the wars of independence (1519-1821)
comadre	midwife, godmother
comandancia general	commanding general
comandante	military commander
comandante general	commanding general created as an agency in 1776

compañia	military unit; a legal association or society of several persons united for a single purpose (commercial, social, ecclesiastical).
comparecer	to appear officially before someone (e.g., a judge, civil register secretary, or notary).
compraventa	contract of purchase and sale
compromiso	pledge, commitment, promise
comunidad	community, particularly a religious group; village, commune
concejo/concejil	council
concierto	agreement, contract, arrangement, settlement
concuñado/da	spouse of one's own spouse's brother or sister

confirmación	confirmation (religious sacrament)
congregación	congregation; assembly; religious brotherhood; committee of cardinals or of a religious order; town or settlement.
conocido	know
conquistadores	Spanish conquerors of the New World in the sixteenth century.
consanguinidad	consanguinity; kinship; blood relationship
consejero	counselor, advisor
Consejo de Castilla or Real	Council of Castille, Royal Council (supreme administrative body in Spain).

Consejo de Indias	Royal council that governed the colonies
consentimiento	consent, compliance, acquiescence
consorte de	spouse, partner, associate
constar	to be recorded or registered
contratación	making a contract; trade
Casa de la Constratación	Spanish governmental entity located in Seville that handled the economic and commercial affairs of the American colonies (1503-1790).
contrato	contract; agreement enforceable by law
contrayente	contracting party, such as in a marriage
contribución	tax
convenio	agreement, convent, pact

convento	community of religious men or women (convent)
cónyuge	spouse, consort, marriage partner
copia literal	literal or word-for-word copy
corregidor	magistrate, an administrator of a city or district
corriente	current, present (week, month, year)
cosa	thing, something; affair, business
coyote	blood mixture (Spanish 4 parts, Indian 3 parts, Negro 1 part); term used on parish registers of Mexico
criollo/a	Creole; Latin-American colonial born of European parents

crisma	chrism, consecrated oil
cuadra	stable; city block
Cuaresma	Lent; collection of Lent sermons
cuarteado	blood mixture (Spanish 2 parts, Indian 1 part, Negro 1 part); offspring of mestizo and mulatta
cuarteron	blood mixture (Spanish 3 parts, mulatta 1 part); at times called morisco
cuate/ta	in Mexico, the word used for twins
cuatrero	blood mixture (Spanish 1 part, Indian 3 parts); offspring of mestizo and Indian
cuatrillizos	quadruplets
cuenta	account, bill, report

cuerpo	body; volume, book, body of laws
cuñada	sister-in-law
cuñado	brother-in-law
cura	parish priest
curato	parish
curia	administrative and judicial organization under the bishop
dado	as long as; provided that; given that
de los mismos	of the same (usually refers to previous wording, such as month and year)
de repente	suddenly
declaración	declaration, statement; affidavit
defensor	defense, counsel
defunción	death

demanda	demand; claim
depósito	deposit; depository
desconocido	unknown
despachar	to finish or shorten at a section; to resolve or determine the causes; to send a person or thing
dicho/cha	declaration, statement; said, the above mentioned; (law) declaration made by a witness
difunto/ta	deceased, dead
digo	I say (frequently used by scribes in records to correct errors as they wrote)
diligencia matrimonial	premarital investigation conducted by a parish priest

diócesis	diocese (unit of Catholic Church presided over by a bishop)
diputado	deputy
directorio	directory
dispensa matrimonial	exception to Canon Law regulation given by a bishop to a bride and groom to permit marriage
dista/distante/distancia	distance (from)
distrito	district
doctrina	doctrine; a district under a priest to indoctrinate Indians; Mexican parish
documento nacional de identidad	personal identity document issued by the civil government

Don	title of respect prefixed to Christian names (usually referred to nobility or office holders before 1832)
Doña	female version of Don; lady; woman
donación	donation, gift, grant
dotación	endowment, dowry
dote	dowry (property brought into marriage by a woman)
ducado	gold coin created by the Catholic Monarchs, originally equivalent to 375 maravedis
ducado de plata	silver ducato
eclesiástico	ecclesiastical
edad	age
ejecutor/ra	executor

emancipación	emancipation (the act of freeing from servitude)
embarcar	to pack, crate, bale; to go aboard a vessel
emigración	emigration
encomendero	Indians assigned to him in an encomienda during early colonial era
encomienda	patronage; commandaery; territory of Indians under an encomendero
entierro	burial, funeral, internment
episcopal	of the bishop
escribanía	notary office; court clerkship; writing desk
escribano	notary; court clerk; judge's secretary

escritura	writing, handwriting; document, deed, instrument, contract
español/la	individual born of Spanish parents in peninsular Spain or in colonial records
español criollo	Spanish creole; individual born of Spanish parents within the colonies
esposo/sa	spouse
estado	status (e.g., marital); state, nation, country; government
estancia	livestock ranch
este	east
exhumación	exhumation
expediente	written proceeding of a particular action; petition; file
explorador	Indian scout or auxiliary

expósito	abandoned, foundling child (frequently used as surname)
expuesto	exposed
extracto del certificado	summary or abstract of a certificate
extrema unción	extreme unction (last rites)
falleció	died
familia	family
familiar	pertaining to a family; domestic; servant of clergy; loyal representative of Inquisition
fecha	date
feligrés/a	parishioner
feligresía	parish; district of a parish
fianza	deposit, guarantee, bond, bail
finca	small farm or ranch
fichas	index cards

fichero	filing cabinet; index card system, filing system, card catalog
filiación	military register of a soldier; parental ties between parents and children
filial	relating to a son; dependent institution
firmo	I sign
folio	page of a book, notebook, or bundle
fornicación	fornication (sexual union outside marriage)
fue	was
fueron	were
gemelas	twin girls
gemelos	twin boys or fraternal twins
gobernación	government, governing

gobernador	governor
grado	degree, grade, rank
gran	grand, great, large
guardia	guard, body of soldiers; keeper, custodian
guía	guide; advisor, instructor, trainer
habitante	inhabitant
hace y dos años	two years ago
hacendado	owner or holder of a hacienda
hacienda	farmstead; a large privately owned estate of rural nature
hacienda de beneficio	mining smelter or factory, a mill farm, or ranch
hacienda de campo	farm or ranch
herederos	heirs
hermandad	brotherhood; confraternity; fraternity; sisterhood

hermano/na	brother/sister
hermano/na carnal	brother/sister, born of the same parents
hermano/na político/ca	brother-in-law/sister-in-law
hidalgo/ga	noble; of noble blood, gentry
hijo/ja	son/daughter, child
hijo/ja adoptivo/va	adopted son/daughter, child
hijo/ja legitimo/ma	legitimate son/daughter, a child born of a legal union
hijo/ja natural	common-born child, illegitimate child (parents could have been legally married)
hijo/ja político/ca	son-in-law/daughter-in-law
hijuela	document listing the assets a person is to receive from a dependent's estate; little daughter, little girl

hoja de servicio	government service record
hipoteca	mortgage, pledge
historía	history; story
hoja	leaf, sheet of paper, page of a book
hoja de servicios	service records, document containing the personal and professional antecedents of government employees
hoy	today
iglesia	church
igual	equal
ilegítimos	illegitimate
immigración	immigration
impedimento	obstacle, hindrance, obstruction (especially in Canon Law, prevents marriage)

imponible	taxable
incógnito/ta	unknown, unrecognized
indemnidad	indemnity, security or protection against injury, damage, or loss
Indias	Indies; the Americas, including México, Central and South America, and the Caribbean
índice	written index, list, catalog
Indio/dia	Indian (Native American)
Indios bárbaros	wild, uncivilized Indians (Native Americans)
infante(a)	infant
información matrimonial	bundle of papers from pre-marriage proceedings, including banns, declarations, baptismal records

infrascrito/ta	written hereafter; undersigned person
inhumación	burial
instancia	petition, request
intendencia	superintendent; administration; intendancy; territorial division under the direction of the Intendente
intestado	intestate, without testament; deceased without a will
inventario	inventory; list
inventario de bienes de	inventory of a deceased person's assets
investigador	investigating, researching; investigator
izquierda	left
jornalero	day laborer

juez	judge, juryman; governor of Castille
juizo de orfaos	court records of orphans
junta	meeting of officials
juramento	oath
jurisdicción	jurisdiction; boundary; district
juros	right of perpetual ownership, perpetual annuity; pension
justicia	justice, rightness, fairness, court (of justice), tribunal
juzgado	local court
la	the (feminine)
labor	cultivated field
labrador	farmer
ladino/na	Ethnic Spanish, Indian, Spanish speaking (mixed blood: Spanish and Indian)

lasto	receipt given to a person who pays for someone else
latifundia	large landed estate (typical in Andalucia, Mexico)
legajo	bundle of loose papers tied together due to a common subject
legitima	legitimate (female)
legitimo	legitimate (male)
legua	league (three and a half miles)
lengua	language, tongue
liberación	exoneration, exemption from taxes or obligations
libertad	freedom, liberty; privilege, right
libramiento	deliverance; warrant or order of payment

libraza	draft; bill of exchange; money order
libro de actos	minute book
libros sacramentales	parish registries
licencia	permission, authority; leaves, furlough
licenciado	release; licensed, holding a degree (master's degree)
limite/limita	limit, boundary
limpieza de sangre	purity of blood (used to show ancestry free of Moors, Jews, Africans in Inquisition records)
liquidación	liquidation, winding up; liquidation of debts
lobo/loba	blood mixture: Indian (1 part) and negro (3 parts)
lonja	public exchange, market

lugar	village, hamlet; place, spot, site
madrastra	step-mother
madre	mother
madre política	mother-in-law, step-mother
madrina	godmother
magistratura	judgeship
mancipación	transfer of property
mandas	bequests
manifestado	manifesting
Mar del norte	the North Sea; the Atlantic and the Caribbean Oceans
Mar del sur	the South Sea; the Pacific Ocean
margen	margin
marido	husband
marina	Navy
marino	sailor

marítima/mo	maritime
marques	marquis (lord over frontier lands; noble title)
mas	more
materno/na	maternal; pertaining to the mother's family
matrimonial	matrimonial; relating to marriage
matrimonio	marriage
mayorazgo	family estate
medio hermano/na	half-brother/half-sister
mejora	special bequest; additional bequest; development, improvement
mellizo/za	twin
memoria	memory, recollection; report; study account

menor	younger, youngest; smaller, smallest
menos	less
merced de tierra	land grant
meritos	merits; accomplishments
mes	month
mestizo/za	person of mixed race (usually Spanish and Indian)
militar	pertaining to the military or war; person serving in the army
mismo	the same; as expressed; equal
monasterio	monastery
moneda	public auction; clearance sale
morador	resident
moreno/na	ethnic Spanish, Indian, negro (mixed blood: Spanish, Indian, and negro)

morisco/ca	Moorish (baptized Moors, mixture of Spanish and mulatto)
mozo/za	single, unmarried; bachelor/bachelorette; young man/young woman
muerte	death
mujer	woman; wife
municipal	relating to a municipality
municipio	municipality; territorial jurisdiction governed by a town council
murió	died
mutuo	mutual
nacer	to be born
nacimiento	birth
nació	was born

natural	native of; born in a given locality; born outside of the marriage contract
naturaleza	nature; nationality; place of origin
nave	ship; nave, aisle
nacesidad	necessity; need
negro/gra	black or dark-skinned; native of various tribes of Africa
negro fino	ethnic Spanish, negro (blood mixture: Spanish 1 part and negro 3 parts; offspring of mulatto and negro)
nombramiento	appointment; election; nomination; commission
nombre de pila	Christian name (name given at baptismal font)
nordeste	Northeast

noroeste	Northwest
norte	North
notable	notable, noteworthy, outstanding
notario	notary
nuera	daughter-in-law
nuestro/tra	our; of ours; ours
Nueva España	colonial Mexico
Nueva Extremadura	the territory of Coahuila, Mexico
Nueva Galicia	colonial Aguascalientes, Jalisco, and parts of Durango, Zacatecas, Nayarit, San Luis Potosí, Coahuila
Nueva Navarra	the Californias in the early colonial period
Nueva Vizcaya	separated from Nueva Galicia; Sinaloa, Sonora, Durango,

	Chihuahua, and parts of Coahuila, Mexico
Nuevo León	Nuevo León, Mexico and its surrounding areas, including part of Tamaulipas
Nuevo Santander	the northern part of colonial Colombia; northeastern Tamaulipas, Mexico, and part of Texas pre-1848
nupcias	nuptials
obispado	bishopric, episcopate
obispo	bishop
óbito	natural death
obituario	obituary
obligación	obligation, responsibility, duty; liability, bond
obras pias	foundation or donation for church or charitable works

oeste	West
oficialía	office or district of the civil register
oficio	occupation; job; work; craft; trade; office; post; position; written communication
oidor	magistrate in the royal courts (audiencia) who heard and sentenced disputes and lawsuits
ojo de agua	spring or waterhole
óleo	blessed oil used in church ceremonies
originario	native of a given place
oro	gold
otorgar	to set forth, establish, offer, grant, stipulate, or promise (usually in legal documents)

otrosi	furthermore, besides, moreover; (law) additional petitions after the principal one
padrastro	step-father
padre	father; priest
padres	parents; ancestors
padre político	father-in-law; step-father
padres no conocidos	parents unknown
padrino	godfather
padrinos	godparents
padrón	census
país	country
paisano	countryman; a Spanish settler
panteón	cemetery; funeral monument where the dead are buried
paraje	stopping place or small village

pardo/da	ethnic Spanish, Indian, negro (blood mixture: Spanish 1 part, Indian 2 parts, negro)
parecer	to appear, seem, look; manner of viewing
parentesco	relationship
párroco	parish priest
parroquia	parish church; the spiritual jurisdiction of a parish priest
parte	part, fragment; share, portion; party to a transaction
partición	division, partition, separation (especially of assets after death)
partido judicial	judicial district, usually covering several villages in a province
párvulo/la	small child

pasado	past
paterno/na	paternal; from the male line
pedimiento	petition; claim presented to a judge in legal cases
peninsular	people born in Spain or Portugal
perdón	pardon; forgiveness; grace; reprieve
permuta	exchange (often of public or ecclesiastical offices); barter
peso	weight; Spanish coin used in the colonies
petición	petition or application filed with a court or government/ ecclesiastical entity
pie	foot; length measurement equivalent to 28 cm in Castille

pieza de indias	a slave in good condition; sometimes refers to young slaves or women in poor condition
plata	silver
plaza	town square or open area in the center of a town
plazo	term, period of time; installment
pleitos	lawsuit, court or judicial action
población	population
poblador	founder or original settler
poder	power; strength; power of attorney; authority
político/ca	by marriage (e.g., padre político = father-in-law)

por	by, for, through, along, via, about, in exchange for, multiplied by
por palabras	by word
posesión	possession; property; estate
postura	posture, position; agreement; bet, wager
prelado	prelate, ecclesiastical dignitary; superior of a convent
presbítero	priest
presente	present, current
presidente	head or leader of the courts (audiencias); one of the titles of the viceroy
presidio	military fortress
pretendiente	claimant; petitioner; candidate; suitor

previsto	anticipated
primo/ma	cousin (child of an aunt or uncle)
primo/ma carnal	first cousin
primogénito	firstborn
privilegio	privilege; grant; concession; exemption; patent
probanza	proof, evidence (especially in legal contexts)
proceso	process; trial; lawsuit; legal action
prohijación	adoption of a child as one's own
promesa	promise, offer; vow, pledge
prorrogación	extension or postponement for a specified time
protesta	protest, declaration, affirmation

protesto	declaration before a notary (to protect rights if a letter of exchange is not paid)
protocolo	book generated and preserved by notary publics
provincia	province
Provincias Internas	Northern Internal Provinces
próximo	next
pueblo	small unincorporated town
pueblo de Indios	Indian (Native American) town
quinceñera	celebration of a female's fifteenth birthday, marking her transition to womanhood
ranchería	Indian (Native American) campsite or temporary settlement
rancho	small, privately owned farm

ratificación	ratification; confirmation
real	royal, pertaining to the Crown; coin of value of 34 maravedíes; a mining town
real audiencia	supreme court or tribunal of the colonial Americas. *The court of last resort. The court served as a representative of the kings, in which its decisions were final, and only the king could reverse them.*
rebisabuelo/a	great-great grandparent
rebisnieto/a	great-great grandchild
recepción - Reception, receiving, receipt; admission; (law) examination of witnesses.	reception, receiving, receipt

recibo - Receipt, document acknowledging payment.	receipt
reclamación - Claim, demand; objection, protest, complaint; (law) remonstration.	claim, demand
reconocimiento - Recognition, admission, acknowledgment; inspection, examination.	recognition, admission
redención - Redemption, salvation; redemption of a pledge, mortgage, etc.	redemption, salvation

reducción - A village of Indians converted to Christianity, usually directed by a religious order such as the Jesuits.	reduction
regidor	alderman of a town
regimento	military unit headed by a colonel
registro - Registration, registry; examination, inspection, search; entry, record; register.	register, record, record book
registros parroquiales	parish registers
reglamento	body of regulations; regulation
reino	kingdom; realm

religioso/sa - One who has taken the vows of an order (i.e., monk, priest, or nun).	religious
renta - Income; rent; annuity; government bonds, public debt.	revenue
renunciación/renuncia - Renunciation; resignation; (law) waiver, disclaimer.	renunciation; resignation
repartimiento - The assessment of work assignments and the subsequent distribution of those to be assigned to their work stations	distribution of lands

in mines, haciendas, public works.	
repudiación	repudiation
requerimiento - Request, requisition, demand, summons; (law) injunction.	request, requisition, demand
resquardo - Protection, shelter; security, voucher; frontier customs guard.	protection, shelter
residencia - Investigation of a colonial official at the end of his term.	investigation of colonial official
residente	resident
retatarabuelo	great-great-great-grandfather
revista	review, inspection of troops

revocación - Revocation, abrogation; annulment; (law) reversal.	revocation, annulment
rey	king
riachuelo	stream
río	river
sacramento - Sacrament (e.g. baptism, marriage, etc.) Sacrament, Eucharist.	sacrament
sacristán - Sexton; the individual who took care of church property, including cemeteries.	sacristan
sala	parlor, hall, court

santo/ta - Holy, saintly, hollowed, sacred, blessed; saint.	holy, saintly
secretarío/ría	the office secretary
segundo/da	second, secondary
seguridad - Safety, security; certainty, assurance; surety bond.	safety, security
seguro/ra - Safe, secure, steady; insurance, insurance policy; permit, warrant.	safe
señalamiento - Designation; appointment; indication (of place, time).	designation; appointment
señorio	domain
septentrion/al	northern

sepultura - Internment, burial; tomb, grave; burial place, sepulcherre.	burial, grave
servicio - Service, serving; voluntary donations given to a king or state; emergency direct tax.	service
signatura - Filing mark (to facilitate filing of documents), library number; Roman Catholic court of justice and pardons.	filing mark
sínodo - Ancient name given to the	ancient name

ecclesiastical councils of a diocese.	
situación/situado/a	location
sobrino/na	nephew/niece
sobrino-bisieto/ta	great-grandnephew/niece
sobrino-nieto/ta	grandnephew/niece
solar	a plot of land given to an individual
soldada - Salary, wages; soldier's pay.	salary, wages
soldadera	female soldier
soldado	soldier
solemnemente	solemnly
soltero/ra	single, unmarried
subrogación	subrogation, substitution
sudeste	southeast
sudoeste	southwest
suegro/a	parent-in-law

sufragáneo	suffragan
sur	south
sustitución - Substitution (usually an agreement for one man to fulfill the military service of another).	substitution
tarjeta - Card (visiting, personal or invitation card; index card, etc.; heading; title (on a map).	card
tasación - Appraisal; appraisement; valuation	appraisal; valuation
tasador	public appraiser
tatarabuelo/la	great-great-grandparent
tataranieto/ta	great-great-grandchild

teniente - Assistant, deputy, substitute; (military) lieutenant.	assistant, deputy
tercero/ra	third; third party
término - Term, word, expression; end, finish, conclusion; limit, boundary; landmark; time limit, term, period, space of time; district.	term, word, expression
territorio/territorial	territory
testador - Testator (person who writes or dictates a will).	testator
testamentario - A person who oversees distribution of dependents assets in	executor

accordance with last will and testament.	
testamento abierto/nuncupativo - Will that is dictated by a dying person before witnesses and recorded by the notary in his/her protocolo.	nuncupative will
testamento cerrado - A will that is written in secret and sealed before a notary and witnesses, to be opened after the testator's death.	closed will
testamento ológrafo - A will that is written and	holographic will

signed in the hand of a testator.	
testamento - A document in which one declares his/her last will and disposes of property.	will
tierra	land
tío	uncle
tío carnal - Cousin of an individual's father or mother (first cousin removed).	cousin of father/mother
tío-abuelo/la - The brother/sister of an individual's grandparent.	granduncle

tío-bisabuelo/la - The brother/sister of the great-grandparent.	great-granduncle/aunt
título - Caption, heading; section (laws and regulations); (law) title of nobility; diploma.	title
traducción	translation
transacción - Transaction, negotiation; settlement, agreement, compromise.	transaction
traspasos - Transfers of property not involving a sale.	property transfers

tributo - Tribute, tax; respect.	tribute, tax
trinidad	trinity
trueco	trade
tutela - Guardianship	guardianship
tutor - Guardian	guardian
universidad	university
ut supra - Latin term meaning "as above."	Latin term 'as above'
valle	valley
véase	look at
vecindad – Neighborhood; local area	neighborhood
vecindario - Persons residing in the same vicinity; list or census of residents.	residents of vicinity

vecino/na - Head of household, a citizen.	head of household, citizen
velación - Vigil, watch; veiling ceremony of a bride and groom in nuptial mass.	vigil, watch
velado/da - Veiled; having received the velación.	veiled
venta	sale
vicario - Religious functionary who takes full charge in the absence of a superior.	vicar
vicario general - The alternate bishop or assistant to the chief	vicar general

judge of diocesan courts.	
villa - A frontier town with its own council and coat of arms.	frontier town
virreinato - The territory governed by a viceroy.	viceroyalty
virrey - Personal representative of the king in colonial America.	viceroy
viruela - Smallpox	smallpox
viático - Traveler's pass; (Catholic Church) last rites; fee, expense money, mileage allowance.	traveler's pass

viuda - Widow	widow
viudo	widower
vecino	neighbor

Chapter 5

International Research

Strategies

Researching Hispanic genealogy internationally can be both rewarding and challenging due to the historical migrations, colonial records, and diverse regions involved. These resources should greatly aid in building an international genealogy, allowing you to trace back ancestors through the complex history and diverse cultures of the Hispanic world. Here are some essential resources and strategies to aid in international Hispanic genealogy research:

When researching Hispanic genealogy beyond national borders, consider these strategies:

1. Leverage International Archives and Libraries

Visit or Contact Directly: If possible, visit foreign archives and libraries to access original documents. If not, contact them directly to request copies or information.

Many Latin American Countries have Archives and Libraries that now have robust websites. I logged on to the Saltillo, Coahuila, Mexico state Archives website and opted to read it in English, this was quite helpful to navigate all available services via their website.

Online Resources: Explore online catalogs and databases of international archives and libraries.

Genealogy Societies: Connect with genealogy societies in the countries where your ancestors lived. They may have specialized resources and knowledge.

(See Chapter 6 for list of Resources)

2. Utilize International Genealogy Websites

FamilySearch.org: This free resource offers a vast collection of international records, including many from Hispanic countries.

Ancestry.com and MyHeritage: These commercial websites also have extensive collections of international records.

Country-Specific Websites: Look for websites dedicated to genealogy in specific Hispanic countries.

3. Explore Digital Collections

Google Books: Search for digitized books, newspapers, and other historical documents that may contain information about your ancestors.

Digital Archives: Many countries have digitized archives that offer access to historical records online.

4. Connect with Other Researchers

Online Forums: Participate in online forums and communities dedicated to Hispanic genealogy.

Genealogy Societies: Join genealogy societies in both your home country and the countries where your ancestors lived.

DNA Testing: Consider DNA testing to connect with potential relatives and learn more about your family's origins.

5. Consider Language Barriers

Translation Services: Use professional translation services for important documents. Other options, Deedl.com translator or Google Translator

6. Understand Immigration Patterns

Identify Departure and Arrival Points: Determine the ports or border crossings your ancestors used.

Explore Passenger Lists: Search passenger lists for ships or trains that traveled between countries.

7. Be Patient and Persistent

Research Can Be Time-Consuming: International research often requires patience and persistence.

By combining these strategies, you can effectively navigate international research and uncover valuable information about your Hispanic ancestors.

Chapter 6

Using Technology and Online Resources

Embracing Technology in the Pursuit of Your Hispanic Heritage

Technology has made it possible to uncover even the most elusive details about your Hispanic ancestors. From digitized records to DNA testing and online communities, these tools open the door to the past, revealing the rich and diverse stories that form the foundation of your identity. The journey is one of discovery, not just of names and dates, but of the cultures, places, and events that shaped your family's history.

Preserving and Sharing Your Family's Story

With every discovery, you document your findings, building a digital family tree that spans continents and centuries. You scan old photos, upload documents, and even record oral histories from older relatives, using cloud services like **Google Drive** or **Dropbox** to preserve them.

Eventually, you compile your research into a family history book. Using tools like **Blurb**, **Ancestry**, **Geni** **or** **Shutterfly,** you create a beautifully bound volume that tells the story of your Hispanic heritage—complete with photos, maps, and family stories. Sharing this book with relatives sparks new interest in their ancestry and brings your family closer together.

DNA Testing: Adding Genetic Insight to Your Research

To dig deeper, you decide to take a DNA test. Services like **23andMe** or **AncestryDNA** can reveal your ethnic makeup, often highlighting regions like Indigenous Americas, Spain, and North Africa, reflecting the complex history of Hispanic populations. Your DNA test reveals a surprising amount of Basque ancestry, leading you to research the migration of Basques to Latin America. Furthermore, these platforms allow you to connect with distant relatives who share your DNA. You receive a message from someone in Mexico or Spain who turns out to be a fourth cousin, providing new clues about your family's migration during the early 20th century.

Genealogy Resources:

Important Notice:

The genealogy resources and links provided in this book are intended to assist you in your family history research. While these links were active and accurate at the time of publication, websites may change, move, or become inactive over time. I do not assume responsibility for the continued availability of these links. Please explore alternative sources or updated URLs as needed for your research.

California

1. Bancroft Library

The Spanish Borderlands and Northern Mexico

The Borderlands are a primary collecting area for The Bancroft Library, which holds manuscripts related to exploration and settlement of the territories from Florida to California.Documents relating to Nueva Vizcaya and the Provincias Internas include records of the Jesuit and Franciscan orders; materials from the Pinart Collections from New Mexico, Chihuahua, Sonora, and other Northern Mexican states; and the Archives of California. Among the administrators and missionaries represented are many governors of New Mexico and California, numerous viceroys, and missionaries and explorers such as Nicolás de

Cardona, Francisco de Ortega, Eusebio Francisco Kino, Pedro Font, Gaspar de Portolá, and Juan Bautista de Anza.

2. **Los Californianos**
3. **Los Pobladores**

4. **LOS FUNDADORES Y AMIGOS DE ALTA CALIFORNIA**

   http://losfundadores.org/exhibits.htm

5. **SOCIETY OF HISPANIC HISTORICAL AND ANCESTRAL RESEARCH**

   http://shhar.net

6. **SOLDADOS Y CALIFORNIOS DE SO. CAL**

We are Southern Californian Living History re-enactors Soldiers and Civilian Californios from 1769 to 1850. We cover Spanish Colonial and Mexican Periods in Alta California. Our state is full of exciting history and our group of re-enactors are dedicated to learning and teaching that history.

http://soldadosycalifornios.webs.com

7. **SOMOS PRIMOS**

Somos Primos is a publication dedicated to past and present articles, events and information concerning Hispanic heritage issues. Somos Primos is an all volunteer effort.

http://www.somosprimos.com

Arizona

Anza Society International

https://anzasociety.org

Colorado

Colorado Society of Hispanic Genealogy (CSHG)
COLORADO SOCIETY OF HISPANIC AMERICA

http://www.hispanicgen.org

Olibama Lopez Tushar Hispanic Legacy Research Center

OLTHLRC promotes an interest in and the study of lives, times, cultures, traditions, ancestries, and histories of the peoples who emigrated to New Spain and New Mexico, many of whom still have descendants in New Mexico, Colorado, California, Texas, Arizona, and Northern Mexico.

http://hispaniclegacy.org

New Mexico

EL PALACIO

http://www.elpalacio.org/

The French in New Mexico
https://frenchinnewmexico.com/

Historical Society of NM https://hsnm.org/

HISPANIC GENEALOGICAL RESEARCH CENTER OF NEW MEXICO (HGRC)

http://www.hgrc-nm.org

NEW MEXICO GENEALOGICAL SOCIETY

https://www.nmgs.org/index.php

info@nmgs.org

NEW MEXICO SOCIETY OF THE SONS OF THE REVOLUTION

http://www.nmssar.org

THE UNIVERSITY OF NEW MEXICO DIGITAL REPOSITORY

New Mexico roots ltd : a demographic perspective from genealogical, historical and geographic data found in the diligencias matrimonies or pre-nuptial investigations (1678-1869) of the Archives of the Archdiocese of Santa Fe : multiple data extracted and here edited in a uniform presentation by years and family surnames

Hispanic Genealogical Research Center

New Mexico State Archives and Libraries

New Mexico State Records Center and Archives

Texas

Hispanic Genealogical Society

Villas Del Norte

http://www.lasvillasdelnorte.com/

www.mexicangenealogy.com

CANARY ISLAND DESCENDANTS' ASSOCIATION(CIDA-SA)

Established in 1977 to honor our ancestor's courage and determination to establish the first municipal government in the Presidio San Antonio de Bejar (Plaza de Armas) where sixteen families of the Canary Islands arrived on the site of the presidio, carrying a royal decree of the King of Spain to establish the first community of Spanish civilians in the area. Departing on March 27, 1730 on a journey that would take them from Santa Cruz, Tenerife, to Havana Cuba and finally landing in Vera Cruz, Mexico and ultimately making the long journey to the Villa de San Fernando on March 9, 1731 www.cida-sa.org

EAST TEXAS HISPANIC GENEALOGY SOCIETY

The East Texas Hispanic Genealogy Society is a group dedicated to finding and sharing information on the families descended from the early settlers and native Americans in Texas, especially in the area of Nacogdoches, Tx.

http://ethgs.org

HISPANIC GENEALOGICAL SOCIETY OF HOUSTON (HGSH)

www.hispanicgs.com

http://www.hispanicgs.org/societies.html

HISPANIC ORGANIZATION FOR GENEALOGY AND RESEARCH (HOGAR) - Texas

www.hogardedallas.com

LOS BEXARENOS GENEALOGICAL AND HISTORICAL SOCIETY

www.losbexarenos.org

LOS PORCIONES GENEALOGICAL SOCIETY

P.O. Box 392

Edinburg, TX 78540

Los Porciones is an organization of genealogy enthusiasts that promotes the long history of Spanish Mexican Texas citizens. The name, Las Porciones, refers to the first Spanish Mexican settlers that came to South Texas and were awarded their land in a "Porcion" or portion or access to the Rio Grande.

https://archives.lib.utrgv.edu/repositories/2/resources/2 64

RIO GRANDE VALLEY HISPANI GENEALOGICAL SOCIETY

A group of friends doing genealogical research at the Family History Center discussed how they believed that if they dug enough, they would find that most Hispanics in the Rio Grande Valley of Texas were related.

www.rgvhispanicgenealogicalsociety.com

SAN ELIZARIO GENEALOGY AND HISTORICAL SOCIETY

Email: saneligenealogy@att.net

TEJANO GENEALOGICAL SOCIETY OF AUSTIN

www.freewebs.com/nosotroslostejanos

If you are researching your Hispanic roots in Texas, check out this group on Facebook

TEXAS TEJANO

www.texastejano.com

VICTORIA HISPANIC GENEALOGICAL AND HISTORICAL SOCIETY OF TEXAS

www.vhghost.com

VILLA DE SAN AGUSTIN - LAREDO GENEALOGY SOCIETY

www.vsalgs.org

Mexico

www.somosancestria.com

Somos is intended for people to get to know their global and Latin American ancestry in a personalized way. SOMOS is a test that determines the genetic ancestry of a person, with a particular emphasis on Latin American ancestry.

Archivo Histórico de Baja California Sur

http://archivohistorico.bcs.gob.mx/presentacion.html

http://www.genealogia.org.mx

http://www.genealogiademexico.com/index.php

ARCHIVO GENERAL DE LA NACION MEXICO

Archivo General de la Nación

difusion@agn.gob.mx

http://www.gob.mx/agn

https://www.gob.mx/agn/en

Mexico - National Archives Directory

Here you can consult general information about the archives located in the different federal entities of the country. This directory demonstrates the diversification and plurality of the types of collections that make up the universe of Mexico's documentary heritage.

MEXICAN REPUBLIC

Aguascalientes

Baja California

Baja California Sur

Campeche

Chiapas

Chihuahua

Ciudad de México

Coahuila

Colima

Durango

Estado de México

Guanajuato

Guerrero

Hidalgo

Jalisco

Michoacán de Ocampo

Morelos

Nayarit

Nuevo León

Oaxaca

Puebla

Querétaro

Quintana Roo

San Luis Potosí

Sinaloa

Sonora

Tabasco

Tamaulipas

Tlaxcala

Veracruz de Ignacio de la Llave

Yucatán

Zacatecas

Facebook:
https://www.facebook.com/groups/mexicangenealogy/

https://mexicangenealogy.info

Index and Transcription to the Census of 1815 for the Province of Texas (San Antonio de Béxar)

NUEVA GALICIA GENEALOGICAL SOCIETY

http://www.nuevagalicia.net/

Mexico Historical Records Collection via LDS

My Heritage

Hispanic Heritage Project

Nuestra Señora de Guadalupe, Paso del Norte-marriage and death records of Juarez and an 1816 census. (Aaron Magdaleno website)

https://mexicangenealogy.com/community/

ASOCIACIÓN LATINOAMERICA DE ARCHIVOS

https://www.facebook.com/Asociación-Latinoamericana-de-Archivos-258339997646620/

GENEALOGICAL STUDIES OF CADEREYTA JIMENEZ, NUEVO LEON, MEXICO

Hispanic surname DNA project

https://www.eagleknight.com

The Genealogy of Mexico

http://garyfelix.tripod.com/index63.html

GUADALAJARA DISPENSAS

http://www.guadalajaradispensas.com

ROOTSPOINT: FONDO COLONIAL

The Fondo Colonial collection of the Archivo Históricos Municipal de Hidalgo del Parral (Parral Archive), spans a period between 1611 and 1821 and contains the civil colonial records of the Province of Nueva Vizcaya, which today consists of the states of Chihuahua, Durango, Sonora, Sinaloa and part of Coahuila. Hidalgo del Parral was the unofficial capital for Nueva Vizcaya for over 100 years, from the 1632s to the 1738s, and has the largest collection of Spanish colonial documents in northern Mexico.

http://www.rootspoint.com/fondo-colonial/

Spain

Here you will find several associations all over Spain:

http://hispagen.es/index.php/contactar

https://guiagenealogica.com/genealogia-mundial/europa/espana.html

https://www.genealogianueva.com/

ASSOCIATIONS

La guía de información genealógica

https://guiagenealogica.com/genealogia-mundial/europa/espana.html

https://www.genealogianueva.com/

Asociación Canaria de Genealogía e Historia Familiar

Asociación Cultural de Genealogía e Historia de Aragón

Asociación de Genealogía Hispana - Hispagen

Una de las webs más veteranas y con información muy detallada que conviene revisar.

Asociación de Genealogía Soriana

Antzinako- Asociación de genealogistas aficionados vasco – navarros
Muy recomendable web si tienes antepasados vasco – navarros.

Asociación de Genealogistas Cantabros - Ascagen
Contiene base de datos y mucha información sobre genealogía en Cantabria.

Asociación de genealogistas gallegos
Contiene base de datos y mucha información sobre genealogía en Galicia, incluye la lista de trabajadores gallegos que fueron a trabajar a Cuba.

Asociación genealógica de Extremadura

Asociación genealógica Riojana - Genrioja

Genealogía e Historia de Familias del País Vasco

Raíces Reino de Valencia

Real Academia Matritense de Heráldica y Genealogía

Sociedad catalana de Genealogía

Sociedad de Estudios genealógicos canarios

PODCASTS / BLOGS

https://open.spotify.com/show/0Cb4lWqQFb3Oo3pDvm
Jc6c

https://elrincondelagenealogia.wordpress.com/about/

https://www.ivoox.com/podcast-historia-
genealogia_sq_f12389972_1.html

SPANISH AMERICAN GENEALOGICAL ASSOCIATION

www.sagacorpuschristi.com

Email: sagacentral@sagacorpuschristi.com

Facebook: https://www.facebook.com/SAGACC2017/

Portal de Archivo Españoles

http://pares.mcu.es

Archivo General de Indias

Documents and maps about the Indies, Spain's mighty empire from the 16th, 17th and 18th centuries, providing the most complete and documented historical view (if not the most objective) of the Spanish administration of the New World.

http://www.andalucia.com/cities/seville/archivo-de-indias.html

New York

HISPANIC GENEALOGICAL SOCIETY OF NEW YORK

http://www.hispanicgenealogy.com

Puerto Rican

http://www.prroots.com

Cyndislist.com

A comprehensive, categorized & cross-referenced list of links that point you to genealogical research sites online.

Cyndi's List has been a trusted genealogy research site for more than 25 years. Cyndi's List is free for everyone to use and it is meant to be your starting point when researching online.

https://www.cyndislist.com/beginners/

Chapter 7

Directory of Ethnic Groups

The Directory of Ethnic Groups in Latin American Colonial Parish Records is a specialized reference tool that genealogists and researchers use to trace family histories and understand the ethnic composition of ancestors during the colonial period in Latin America. These records, maintained by Catholic parishes, are valuable because they often provide detailed information about baptisms, marriages, and burials, and they often include references to the ethnic or racial identity of individuals. Understanding this directory involves recognizing the rich, multi-ethnic societies that formed in Latin America due to colonization, indigenous cultures, African slave labor, and migrations from Europe and Asia.

Here's what the directory typically covers:

1. Ethnic Classifications in Colonial Parish Records

Colonial Latin American societies were racially diverse, and records often classified individuals by ethnicity or racial background. Terms commonly found in these records include:

Peninsulares: Spaniards born in Spain who migrated to the colonies.

Criollos: Descendants of Spaniards born in Latin America.

Indígenas/Indians: Indigenous peoples of Latin America, often classified by specific tribes or regions.

Mestizos: Individuals of mixed European and Indigenous ancestry.

Mulatos: Individuals of mixed European and African ancestry.

Africans/Negros: People of African descent, often enslaved or freed during the **colonial period.**

Zambos: Individuals of mixed Indigenous and African ancestry.

Asian Communities: Though rarer, there were also mentions of Asian immigrants, particularly from the Philippines, due to the Spanish galleon trade.

The directory would offer guidance on how these ethnic terms were used in different regions and time periods, as well as how they might affect the interpretation of genealogical records.

2. Regional Variations and Parish Recordkeeping

Colonial parish records vary significantly depending on the region. The directory helps genealogists understand the regional differences in how ethnic groups were classified and recorded. For example:

In Mexico, parish records might include detailed racial categories like "mestizo" or "castizo" (a term for people with mixed Spanish and Mestizo heritage).

In Peru, parish records might more heavily document the large Indigenous population and African slaves brought for labor in the silver mines.

In Brazil, ethnic classifications often reflected the diverse African slave populations brought to work on sugar plantations, with terms like "Crioulo" (African-born slaves) and "Pardo" (mixed European and African ancestry).

The directory can provide specific tips on accessing archives for these regions, including online databases or libraries that house colonial records.

3. Types of Records and Information Found

Baptismal Records: Baptisms were often the first significant church interaction for individuals. These records usually list the child's ethnicity, along with the parents' names and ethnicity, offering valuable clues about mixed-ethnicity families.

Marriage Records: These records often contain more detailed racial identifiers, especially when the marriage was between individuals of different racial backgrounds. Mixed-race marriages were sometimes noted, reflecting the legal and social complexities of race in colonial society.

Burial Records: These documents often recorded the deceased's ethnicity, especially for enslaved Africans or Indigenous peoples, and might also include the person's status (e.g., free or enslaved).

Chapter 8

Overcoming Common Challenges

You sit down at your desk, prepared to dive into your family's history. You've heard stories passed down from your grandparents—tales of ancestors from Mexico, Spain, and possibly even Cuba. But as you begin to dig deeper into your research, the challenges start to emerge. Or you may hear conflicting family stories from relatives. It's important to keep note of all family stories, so as to consider as you piece together all verified data before adding this family data onto your family tree. Many have come realize that the surname they carry is not the original family surname, only to find out that a distant relative or for other reasons that ancestor was adopted. This is a very common occurrence in genealogy.

1. Language Barriers: Decoding Old Spanish Records

One of the first hurdles you encounter is the language itself. Many of the records you need to trace your ancestors are written in Spanish, and some are in older dialects that are hard to understand. Birth certificates, marriage records, and census forms are often handwritten, making them even more difficult to interpret. You stare at an 18th-century baptismal record, struggling to decipher the faded ink and elaborate script.

Rather than let the language barrier stop you, you take action. First, you use online translation tools, such as Google Translate or Deedl.com, to get a rough idea of the document's contents. Then, you join a Hispanic genealogy forum, where native Spanish speakers and experienced genealogists help you interpret the historical context and terms used in the records. Gradually, you become familiar with common phrases, abbreviations, and old-fashioned terminology.

2. Navigating Name Variations and Surnames

As you continue your research, you notice something puzzling: your ancestors' names seem to change from record to record. Sometimes they are listed with their full paternal and maternal surnames (following the Hispanic naming convention), while other times only one surname appears. Adding to the confusion, some names are spelled differently across different documents. For example, your ancestor's surname, "González," is sometimes spelled "Gonsalez."

You realize that name variations and inconsistent record-keeping were common in past centuries. To overcome this, you expand your search to include different variations of your ancestors' names. You also start researching naming conventions used in different Hispanic countries, learning that some regions have unique practices, such as double surnames or the use of religious titles in place of family names. Understanding these cultural norms helps you identify the correct individuals in your family tree, even when the records seem inconsistent.

3. Locating Elusive Records: Church vs. Civil Registrations

Another challenge comes when you try to find specific birth or marriage records. In some cases, civil registration only began in the late 19th or early 20th century in certain Hispanic countries, and earlier records were maintained by the Catholic Church. You realize that the documents you're looking for might be hidden in baptismal registries or marriage records held in parish archives that have not yet been digitized.

Instead of giving up, you get creative. You contact local parishes in the region where your ancestors lived and inquire about their records. Sometimes this means sending emails or even making phone calls in Spanish. You also tap into resources like FamilySearch and PARES (Spain's digital archive) or Mexico's Archivos General de la Nacion which are actively digitizing church records. When records aren't immediately available online, you add those parishes to your list of places to visit in person during your next family trip.

4. Understanding Migration Patterns and Border Changes

Your next obstacle is piecing together your family's migration history. You know your ancestors lived in Mexico for generations, but family lore suggests they originally came from Spain. To complicate matters, you find a 19th-century record showing that some of your relatives moved to the United States.

As you dig deeper, you learn that understanding historical migration patterns is key to tracing Hispanic ancestry. Wars, colonialism, and economic changes all influenced the movement of people between Spain, Latin America, and the U.S. You research the Spanish colonization of the Americas, the migration of Basques to Mexico, and the Bracero Program, which brought Mexican workers to the U.S. in the 1940s.

Armed with this historical context, you expand your search to include passenger lists, border crossing records, and naturalization documents. These reveal the paths your ancestors took over time, helping you understand why they migrated and where they settled.

5. Dealing with Gaps in Records and Oral Histories

As you trace your family back further in time, you hit a major roadblock: missing records. Wars, fires, and poor record-keeping practices mean that some vital documents simply no longer exist. And while oral histories passed down through your family are helpful, they are often incomplete or filled with conflicting information.

Faced with these gaps, you turn to alternative sources. You explore land deeds, military records, and even old newspapers, looking for any mention of your ancestors. You also interview older family members, piecing together bits of oral history that could point to new leads. Through persistence and creativity, you start filling in the gaps, even when the paper trail has run cold.

6. Breaking Through Brick Walls with DNA Testing

After months of research, you hit a brick wall. There are still questions about your family's origins that you can't answer. That's when you decide to take a DNA test. Services like AncestryDNA and 23andMe offer insights into ethnic ancestry, and you hope they can help you confirm family stories about Indigenous, Spanish, and possibly African roots.

When the results come in, you're astonished. Your DNA confirms Spanish ancestry, but also shows traces of North African and Indigenous heritage, reflecting the complex cultural and historical makeup of Hispanic communities. Even more exciting, the test connects you with distant cousins in Spain, Mexico and Argentina. By reaching out to them, you uncover new family records and share discoveries that help break through the final brick walls in your research.

Conclusion: Embracing the Journey of Discovery

In the end, your journey to uncover your Hispanic ancestors wasn't easy, but the challenges you faced made each discovery even more meaningful. With persistence, creativity, and the use of modern tools like DNA testing, online databases, and historical resources, you've pieced together a rich, vibrant family history. More than just dates and names, you've gained a deeper understanding of where you come from—and with it, a sense of connection to the generations that came before you.

Now, when you look at old family photos or visit ancestral towns, you do so with a profound appreciation for the stories and struggles that shaped your Hispanic heritage. Through hard work and determination, you've brought the past to life, preserving it for future generations to discover.

Chapter 9

Genealogy Tools Must Haves

Genealogy Software

<u>EasyGenie.org</u>: custom genealogy charts have clean designs and easy-to-read fonts, with lots of space to record genealogy data such as names, dates, immigration data, hometowns, citations, and other genealogy information.

Whether you're an amateur family history sleuth, a professional genealogist, or looking for genealogy tools. EasyGenie had all the tools needed to start your genealogy journey.

<u>Family Tree Maker</u>: Popular for building detailed family trees and syncing with online databases.

<u>Legacy Family Tree:</u> Offers robust features for tracking genealogical information.

Gramps: Free, open-source software for documenting ancestry.

Online Genealogy Databases

Ancestry.com: Provides access to census records, immigration data, and more.

FamilySearch: A free service with vast records from around the world.

MyHeritage: Focuses on European and Latin American genealogical records.

Findmypast: Great for tracking Hispanic roots.

Translation Tools

Google Translate: For translating Spanish, Portuguese, and Latin records.

DeepL: Offers higher accuracy in translations of historical documents.

Document Organization Tools

Evernote/OneNote: For saving and organizing your findings.

Dropbox/Google Drive: Cloud storage for digitizing and storing important documents.

YourLegacyYourStory.com

Your Legacy YourStory was born from a group deeply involved in the archiving and digitizing industry. After years of scanning film and videotapes, we found our customers' lives and ancestors were full of great stories. We helped many memories be preserved and passed down, but the stories often remained untold. As we were asked again and again to make family history books and documentaries, our team of creative and talented people developed a new path forward as professional storytellers.

Map Tools

Google Earth: For locating historical sites tied to family history.

Mapire: Provides historical maps that can help trace geographical changes.